Bright
≡**Summaries**.com

AF143859

The Barber of Seville

BY BEAUMARCHAIS

BOOK ANALYSIS

Written by Annabelle Falmagne and Hélène Dupuis
Translated by Emma Hanna

The Barber of Seville

BY BEAUMARCHAIS

PIERRE BEAUMARCHAIS

FRENCH PLAYWRIGHT, POET, POLITICIAN AND MUSICIAN

- **Born in Paris in 1732.**
- **Died in Paris in 1799.**
- **Notable works:**
  - *Eugénie* (1767), play
  - *The Marriage of Figaro* (1784), play
  - *The Guilty Mother* (1792), play

Pierre-Augustin Caron was born in 1732 and is best known by the surname he later adopted, Beaumarchais, which is derived from "le Bois Marchais", an area of land that belonged to his wife. He initially followed in the professional footsteps of his father, who was a master watch-maker, before entering Parisian high society in 1759 as a music tutor for the daughters of King Louis XV (1710-1774). He gained a reputation as an incorrigible womaniser during this time, before being made Secretary-Councillor to the King, a position which saw him take on a number of diplomatic responsibilities.

Beaumarchais' first real taste of literary success came in 1775, when his play *The Barber of Seville* was first performed. After falling victim to censorship and the outdated practices of the Comédie-Française (a prestigious French state theatre), in 1777 he founded the *Société des auteurs dramatiques* (Society of Playwrights), which is generally considered to be the origin of the modern idea of copyright. Beaumarchais died in 1799.

THE BARBER OF SEVILLE, OR THE FUTILE PRECAUTION

A LIVELY ROMANTIC COMEDY

- **Genre:** play (comedy)
- **Reference edition:** Beaumarchais, P-A. (1964) *The Barber of Seville and The Marriage of Figaro*. Trans. Wood, J. London: Penguin.
- **1st edition:** 1775
- **Themes:** friendship, love, trickery, disguises, marriage

It may come as a surprise to learn that the first performance of *The Barber of Seville* on 23 February 1775 was a resounding failure. However, Beaumarchais spent three days rewriting the play, reducing its length from five acts to four, and a second performance was held on 26 February. This revised version of the play was much more successful.

The Barber of Seville follows the same dramatic

structure as plays such as *The School for Wives* (1662) by Molière (French playwright, 1622-1673), and tells the story of Count Almaviva, an 18th-century Spanish noble who enlists the help of a barber named Figaro to woo a young woman named Rosine, who is betrothed to her elderly guardian Don Bartholo.

This romantic comedy is best known for the sparkling wit and humorous wordplay of its dialogue, as well as the numerous comic misunderstandings that ensue due to the many disguises adopted by its characters.

SUMMARY

ACT I

Count Almaviva leaves Madrid and heads to Seville in search of a young orphan girl named Rosine, with whom he has fallen madly in love. When the Count arrives in Seville, he lingers outside Rosine's house, where he bumps into his former servant Figaro, who now works as Don Bartholo's barber and apothecary. Figaro tells Rosine that a suitor is waiting outside, and she drops a page of sheet music for a song called *The Futile Precaution* out the window with a note hidden inside asking her suitor to tell her his name. The Count quickly picks up the page, while Bartholo searches through the street for it, seething with jealousy.

Figaro explains the situation to the Count, and describes Don Bartholo, who is a doctor, in less than flattering terms. Figaro also says that he will act as the Count's accomplice, and suggests that the Count disguise himself as a drunken officer so that he can take advantage of Bartholo's hospitality and sneak into the house. They then overhear Bartholo talking about a man named Bazile, who is supposed to arrange Rosine and Don Bartholo's wedding in secret. The Count serenades Rosine, and uses the song to declare his love for her and tell her that his name is Lindor, thus concealing his true identity.

ACT II

Figaro talks to Rosine, who asks him to deliver a letter to her suitor after the barber tells her that he is a friend of Lindor's. Figaro then tries to make it possible for the Count to visit the house by making all of the servants ill, which angers Bartholo. Bartholo also learns that the Count is in Seville through a conversation with Bazile, who advises him to forbid Rosine from seeing any visitors until the next day, when he intends to marry her.

The Count disguises himself as a drunken knight as planned and shows up at Bartholo's house, asking for shelter. He uses this as an opportunity to slip a letter to Rosine, who recognises him as Lindor. However, Don Bartholo is suspicious and claims that he is not required to show soldiers hospitality as a pretext for sending the Count away. He then demands that Rosine let him read the letter she is holding: she initially refuses, then pretends to swoon and switches the message from the Count with a letter from her cousin, which she gives to her guardian, allaying his fears.

ACT III

The Count adopts a second ruse: he returns to Bartholo's home and introduces himself as Alonzo, pretending that Bazile is ill and that he has come to act as a substitute music tutor for Rosine. However, Don Bartholo does not believe him, so the Count gives him the letter Rosine had written to him, in which she declares her affection for him, in order to gain Bartholo's trust, and even pretends that he is spying on Count Almaviva on Bazile's behalf. He also tells Bartholo that if Rosine refuses to marry him, he should tell her that the letter was given to him by the Count's mistress, as this would make her jealous and convince her to reject the lover who has seemingly betrayed her and accept Don Bartholo's advances instead. By this point, he has completely won over Don Bartholo, but the doctor still refuses to give "Alonzo" the letter back, as he wants to use it against Rosine later.

The Count gives Rosine, who has recognised him, a music lesson. Bartholo is still in the room, but the music keeps lulling him to sleep, so the two lovers try to snatch a few moments of private conversation every time he dozes off. Figaro arrives shortly afterwards, and offers to shave the doctor so that the two lovers will be left alone. However, Bartholo refuses to leave the room, and sends the barber to look for his toiletries. This means that he has to give Figaro a bunch of keys, which includes the key to the window. When he returns, Figaro causes a distraction so that the Count can tell Rosine that he will come by that very night and help her to escape through the window. However, another obstacle appears in the form of Bazile, although the Count quickly solves this problem by slipping him a bag full of money. This bribe, coupled with the fact that everyone present (including Bartholo, although he is unaware of the scheme being played out under his nose) is urging him to go and rest, quickly convinces him to leave again. Figaro then begins shaving Bartholo again, but the doctor overhears part of the conversation between the two lovers and realises that the music tutor is an imposter, meaning that the second ruse is also a failure.

ACT IV

Bartholo's suspicions are confirmed when Bazile later admits that the music tutor was actually Count Almaviva in disguise. At this point, the doctor decides to marry Rosine that night, and tricks her into agreeing to the match by showing her the letter that she had sent to her lover and telling her that it was given to him by the Count's mistress. Rosine then tells Don Bartholo about the Count's plan to spirit her away in the night, as they had discussed during the music lesson. A short time later, Figaro and the Count sneak into the house to meet Rosine, but they find that Bartholo, having discovered their plan, has removed the ladder that had been leaning up against the window and gone to look for help. While they are still figuring out what to do, Bazile arrives with a notary, who is supposed to officiate the wedding of Don Bartholo and

Rosine and has therefore brought two unsigned marriage contracts. Since Bartholo has not yet returned, the Count and Rosine take advantage of this brief window of opportunity to get married, with Figaro and Bazile (whom they bribe again) as witnesses. The notary does not realise that the Count is not the man whose wedding he was supposed to officiate until the ceremony is over, at which point Don Bartholo finally returns and is forced to concede defeat in spite of the (futile) precautions he took to ensure his victory over the Count, symbolising the triumph of love over reason.

CHARACTER STUDY

COUNT ALMAVIVA

Count Almaviva is a dashing aristocrat who is hopelessly in love with Rosine and is prepared to do whatever it takes to win her hand in marriage. The Count is shown to be more astute than the lovers in most similar comedies, who tend to be quite naïve – in fact, Figaro's cunning seems to rub off on him over the course of the play.

He does not use his social position to achieve his goals; on the contrary, he spends the entire play fearing that Bartholo will recognise him. Furthermore, he initially decides to hide his true identity from Rosine in order to make sure that she loves him for who he is, and not because of his status as a nobleman. He does not flaunt his youth or title until the end of the fourth and final act of the play, at which point he uses them to prove his superiority to the old doctor, enabling him to marry Rosine at last: "I am a man of rank, young and rich" (Act IV, Scene VIII).

The Count adopts four different identities over the course of the play:

- Count Almaviva, his true identity;
- Lindor, the young suitor who stands underneath Rosine's window;
- Lindor, the drunken officer who asks Bartholo for hospitality;
- Alonzo, Bazile's student and Rosine's substitute music tutor.

Although some of his schemes go awry, his dream of marrying Rosine eventually comes true.

FIGARO

Figaro was a servant in Count Almaviva's employ before his arrival in Seville, where he now works for Don Bartholo as his barber and apothecary. His only goal in life is to find happiness, which is what motivated him to take control of his own fate. His independent spirit is typical of 18th-century philosophy, which was more focused on finding happiness on earth than obeying strict moral codes in the hopes of being rewarded in the afterlife.

Unlike the manservants in many plays, who only help their masters because they are ordered to do so, Figaro is a commoner whose decision to help a noble is entirely of his own volition and motivated by a simple desire to be entertained, rather than avarice or moral convictions.

Despite his youthful energy and the fact that he is often depicted as a young man, Figaro is no longer in his prime, as is proven in Act III, Scene V, when he reels off a long list of his accomplishments from his lengthy professional career.

The character of Figaro seems to bear quite a number of similarities to Beaumarchais himself: they both find amusement in everything around them, and joke even when they are angry, as Figaro notes early in the play: "I forced myself to laugh at everything for fear of having to weep" (Act I, Scene II).

ROSINE

Rosine is a young orphan and the ward of the tyrannical Don Bartholo, who wants to marry her in spite of the enormous age difference between them.

She is a modern, educated woman who is far from ignorant of her suitors' intentions towards her. She also proves to be highly intelligent, such as when she pretends to faint so that she can trick Bartholo into reading an innocent letter that was sent to her by her cousin, instead of the letter from her lover. However, she also has an emotional side, which jeopardises the plan to spirit her out of Bartholo's house when her feelings for the Count are compromised (Act IV, Scene III). However, she and the Count eventually end up together.

DON BARTHOLO

Don Bartholo is a doctor and acts as Rosine's guardian. Figaro describes him as a mistrustful, jealous old man with a spiteful streak, making him a perfect foil for the Count. However, Bartholo's wits have not dulled in his old age, especially when his plans for his young ward are at stake. He is also shown to be extremely reactionary and opposed to all the innovations of the 18th century:

> "BARTHOLO: [...] What a barbarous age! [...] What has it produced that we should praise it?

Nonsense of every kind! Liberty of thought, the Force of Gravity, Electricity and Magnetism, universal toleration, inoculation, quinine, the Encyclopedia, and the newfangled Drama!" (Act I, Scene III)

Furthermore, Bartholo's personality and comments make it clear that he only cares about the money he earns through his work as a doctor, not his patients or their recovery (Act II, Scene XIV). He gets his comeuppance at the end of the play, when his plans fail and Rosine marries the Count instead of him.

DON BAZILE

Don Bazile is Rosine's music tutor and Bartholo's trusted helper; he has even taken full responsibility for organising Bartholo and Rosine's wedding.

Bazile represents everything Figaro hates, namely dishonesty and slander (Act II, Scene VIII and Act IV, Scene I). However, he does possess some common sense, as seen at the start of Act IV when he advises Bartholo not to go through with the wedding, saying that it is a bad idea to marry a woman who does not love you, as this may lead her to be unfaithful in the future. However, these fleeting bursts of good sense never last long, and his greed leads him to unhesitatingly betray Bartholo twice (when "Alonzo" bribes him to keep quiet about his real identity in Act III, Scene XI, and when he agrees to act as a witness at the Count's wedding to Rosine after being offered a second bribe in Act IV, Scene VII).

ANALYSIS

A BLEND OF TRADITION AND INNOVATION

According to René Pomeau, the author of the preface to the French version of *The Barber of Seville*, the quality of the national theatre in France declined steeply in the 18th century, as the authors of tragedy and comedy alike hesitated to fully commit to their chosen art form.

However, this was before Beaumarchais arrived on the scene. His stated goal was to revitalise the art of comedy and to bring light-heartedness back to the French theatre by combining it with a more contemporary sense of humour. In order to achieve this goal, he drew on the works of classic playwrights such as Molière, while also adopting a new, distinctive tone that made his plays entirely his own.

The plot of *The Barber of Seville* is fairly conventional, and concludes with the happy ending that is expected of any comedy, even though

Beaumarchais throws more than a few snares and setbacks in his protagonists' path to keep the audience on their toes. Furthermore, Figaro bears certain similarities to other servant characters in classic comedies, notably the character of Scapin from Molière's play *Scapin the Schemer* (1671), who is similarly ingenious and cunning. He also willingly helps his former master, Count Almaviva, to foil Bartholo's plans and win the heart of Rosine, the woman he loves.

However, Figaro cannot be dismissed as a mere dramatic archetype or a simple manservant. From the very beginning of the play, his character speaks surprisingly freely for someone who is not of noble birth: he is often insolent, and is shown to be even more quick-witted than the Count. In the conversations between the Count and his former servant, which sometimes descend into verbal sparring matches, Figaro always has the last word, which gives him something of an upper hand over his former master: "On the basis of the virtues commonly required in a servant does Your Excellency know many masters who would pass muster as valets?" (Act I, Scene II). As such, he can be described as the play's central character in both word and deed.

Another innovative technique used by Beaumarchais is to develop Figaro's character in a manner almost reminiscent of a novel. Figaro has travelled extensively and tried his hand at a wide variety of different professions, giving him a nuanced backstory, and his personal musings on life and often controversial views on society give him a great deal of psychological depth.

Figaro can also be considered a kind of spokesman or fictional alter-ego for Beaumarchais, given that they have a number of shared experiences. For example, Figaro denounces the censorship he has been subjected to in Act I, Scene II, which is a direct reference to the difficulties Beaumarchais experienced with early performances of *The Barber of Seville*.

Beaumarchais' innovative approach to character development is also in evidence in his subsequent works (namely *The Marriage of Figaro* and *The Guilty Mother*). This enabled him to further develop Figaro's nuanced, complex personality over the course of several years and follow him through various other stages of his life (he is reunited with his parents and gets married, etc.). Beaumarchais' style evolved in tandem with the development of the characters of Figaro, the Count and Rosine, and the tone of his works got darker over time as his characters aged, going from the light-hearted comedy of *The Barber of Seville* to more serious drama in *The Guilty Mother.*

THE ART OF COMEDY

The comic tone of *The Barber of Seville* is one of the work's defining features, and is developed in several ways:

- **Comic characters.** This refers to the inclusion of characters who are "caricatures", such as the valets, or the exaggeration of some of a character's personality traits, such as Bartholo's excessive jealousy and conservatism. There are also amusing contrasts between the names of certain characters and their nature or their attitude; for example, Wakeful is described as "a dull, sleepy boy", while Youthful is an old man.
- **Physical comedy.** For example, in Act II, Scene VII, Wakeful cannot stop yawning and Youthful walks around with the help of a cane.

- **Situational comedy.** This is related to the twists and turns of the plot and the misunderstandings the characters face, and relies on the audience becoming invested in the story, which makes it more satisfying when the characters successfully trick Bartholo. For example, the scene in which Rosine attempts to hide the letter from the Count from Bartholo (Act II, Scene XV) is based on this type of comedy, as is Act III, Scene IV, in which the two lovers declare their love for each other right under Bartholo's nose, using a song called *The Futile Precaution* as cover.
- **Wordplay.** As its name suggests, this type of humour is language-based, and is the predominant type of comedy in this play. Beaumarchais uses many different literary techniques to give his text tremendous richness and humour. For example, it includes:
  - Repetition:
    "THE COUNT: Go straight to bed, my dear Bazile.
    FIGARO: His face is all haggard. Go to bed!
    BARTHOLO: Upon my word! One can diagnose a fever a mile off! Go to bed!
    ROSINE: Why ever did you come out? They say it's infectious. Go to bed!" (Act III, Scene XI)

- Stichomythia (a verbal exchange made up of very short replies):
  "BARTHOLO: I know. Be quiet.
  BAZILE [in a whisper]: Who told you?
  BARTHOLO [whispering]: He did of course.
  THE COUNT [in a whisper]: Of course I did. Now listen.
  ROSINE [whispering to Bazile]: Can you really not keep quiet?" (*ibid.*)

Beaumarchais also uses contrasts, particularly to illustrate Figaro's determination to force himself to "laugh at everything for fear of having to weep". For example:

- Parallels:
  "FIGARO: [...] welcomed in one place and jailed in the next" (Act I, Scene II)
- Antithesis:
  "THE COUNT: [...] You are so fat and sleek...
  FIGARO: Well, what do you expect, Sir – it's poverty." (*ibid.*)

Most of these techniques are flavoured with the irony and sarcasm that are peppered throughout the play's dialogue, which emphasises the work's satirical nature. These techniques also include:

- ◦ Antiphrasis:

  "THE COUNT: Miserable scoundrel! If you utter a single word...

  FIGARO: Yes, I recognize you – and the familiar epithets you always condescended to bestow upon me." (*ibid.*)

- ◦ Exaggeration:

  "BARTHOLO: Yes, but it won't happen again. I'm going to fasten up this lattice.

  ROSINE: Don't stop at that! Wall up the window at the same time! Prison or dungeon – it doesn't make much difference." (Act II, Scene IV)

This wide range of stylistic devices perfectly complements the *The Barber of Seville*'s fast pace, witty dialogue and rich language, and all of these elements combine to form a work which fulfils Beaumarchais' goal of using light-hearted comedy to criticise the failings of contemporary French society, as stated in his preface to the original French version of the play.

THE PLAY'S TITLE

This play has two titles, both of which give us some insight into the author's intentions in writing it.

Firstly, *The Barber of Seville*, the title by which it is best known, refers to Figaro and designates him as the play's main character. Figaro is living in Seville and working for Bartholo as a barber, which gives him access to the doctor's house and means that he is better placed than anyone else to help Count Almaviva with his plans. This title also alludes to Figaro's ingenuity, as he is able to turn almost any situation to his advantage, as he notes himself: "in fair weather and foul, defying all enemies, laughing at my own misfortunes, and playing the barber to anyone who needed me" (Act I, Scene II). In this context, "playing the barber" can be taken to mean "getting the upper hand over someone", and this meaning is even clearer in the original French version. This is likely part of the reason why Beaumarchais chose to make his protagonist a barber.

The play's second title, *The Futile Precaution* (or *The Useless Precaution* in some translations), is a reference to a short story of the same name by Paul Scarron (French writer, 1610-1660), who was one of Beaumarchais' greatest sources of literary inspiration. This title also alludes to all the precautions and schemes Bartholo comes up with in his attempt to ensure that he will be able to marry Rosine, all of which come to naught. It can also be interpreted as the moral of the story, given that Figaro closes the play with the following words: "We may be certain, Doctor, that when youth and love are at one anything that age may do to prevent them can only be described as a futile precaution" (Act IV, Scene VIII). Furthermore, it is used as the title of a play within the play itself, which Rosine throws out the window in order to get a letter to the Count:

> "BARTHOLO: What's the paper you have there?
> ROSINE: Some lines from *The Futile Precaution* which my music master gave me yesterday.
> BARTHOLO: And what is *The Futile Precaution*?
> ROSINE: A new play." (Act I, Scene III)

The titular song of this play, which the Count sings to Rosine while disguised as Alonzo, allows the two lovers to communicate with each other right under Bartholo's nose. *The Futile Precaution* therefore becomes part of Figaro's schemes to help the Count dupe Don Bartholo and marry Rosine, in spite of the elderly doctor's interference.

THE INSPIRATION FOR *THE BARBER OF SEVILLE*

Beaumarchais drew on several sources of inspiration when writing this comedy:

- His own drama **Eugénie**, in which the heroine tries to avoid an arranged marriage with an elderly soldier by embarking on a relationship with a libertine;
- **La Précaution inutile** ("The Futile Precaution", 1655) by Paul Scarron, a short story in which a woman hides her lover in a wardrobe in order to keep her husband from discovering her affair;
- Several works by Molière:
  - **The School for Wives**. This play features several of the same character archetypes as *The Barber of Seville* (for example, the characters of Rosine and Agnes are very alike), a similar situation (an old man wants to marry his young ward) and the same ending (the two lovers get married). However, Beaumarchais introduces a certain degree of novelty through the character of Figaro.
  - **The Bourgeois Gentleman** (1670). Rosine's

surprise when she recognises her suitor while he is disguised as a music tutor is similar to Lucine's surprise when she encounters Cléonte.

- ○ **Scapin the Schemer**. There are a number of parallels that could be drawn between the characters of Scapin and Figaro, as both play the role of the central character and display a great deal of cunning and ingenuity over the course of the play. The main difference between these two characters is the fact that while Scapin is primarily motivated by his desire to exact vengeance against Géronte, Figaro has no ulterior motive for helping the Count. On the contrary, as Beaumarchais says in his preface to *The Barber of Seville*, he is simply a boyish, carefree man who is able to laugh in the face of both success and failure.

- ○ **The Imaginary Invalid** (1673). In this play, the character of Cléante disguises himself as a music tutor in order to get close to Angélique, the object of his affections, much as Almaviva does in *The Barber of Seville*.

However, Beaumarchais sets his work apart through the inclusion of a total of four songs, which make the play a great deal more dynamic and provide the characters with a covert means of communication. After all, it has often been said that music is the language of emotion, so what better conduit could the lovers use to express their feelings for each other? Music therefore plays a significant role in the narrative and is elevated above the status of mere "ambient noise", as it is the only means by which the lovers are able to communicate with each other.

THE AGE OF ENLIGHTENMENT

One of Beaumarchais' goals in writing this play was to defend the ideas of the philosophers of the Age of Enlightenment. This philosophical and intellectual movement emerged in Europe in the 18th century, and aimed to promote and defend the ideals of tolerance, rational thought and civil and individual liberties. The writers of that era, such as Montesquieu (French writer and philosopher, 1689-1755), Voltaire (French writer and philosopher, 1694-1778) and Denis Diderot (French writer and philosopher, 1713-

1784), attempted to use their writing to persuade their peers of the merits of reason and critical thinking in the fields of science, religion and politics, among others. They also firmly believed in humanity's capacity for self-improvement and in the virtue of actively seeking happiness.

In *The Barber of Seville*, Beaumarchais makes his belief in the ideals of the Enlightenment clear in a number of ways:

- He depicts the detractors of the Enlightenment in a highly unflattering light. For example, Beaumarchais makes Bartholo seem ridiculous when he disparages a variety of innovations, which is evidently intended to mock conservatives. This also makes it clear that Beaumarchais supports everything that Bartholo is criticising:

  > "BARTHOLO: [...] What a barbarous age! [...] What has it produced that we should praise it? Nonsense of every kind! Liberty of thought, the Force of Gravity, Electricity and Magnetism, universal toleration, inoculation, quinine, the Encyclopedia, and the newfangled Drama!" (Act I, Scene III)

- Figaro and the Count – who represent Beaumarchais himself – then expound on the core ideals of the Enlightenment, including:
  - seeking happiness is a virtue: "THE COUNT: […] We all run after happiness, and mine lies in Rosine's affection";
  - all men are free;
  - the law must defend the liberty of the weakest members of society against the domination of the most powerful.

It can therefore be said that Beaumarchais was a man of his time, who was entirely of the mind that "Men are born and remain free and equal in rights" (Declaration of the Rights of the Man and of the Citizen of 1789).

CRITICISM OF POWER AND THOSE WHO ABUSE IT

In the preface to *The Marriage of Figaro*, the sequel to *The Barber of Seville*, Beaumarchais explicitly stated that his goal in writing his comedies was to denounce abuse of any kind:

> "Vices and abuses are unchanging, but disguise themselves in thousands of different forms

behind a mask of manners and convention; the noble task of any man who devotes himself to the theatre is to tear away this mask and expose them."[1]

Although Beaumarchais' work was popular with the public, this was no easy task. He often drew heavy criticism as a result, and even faced the threat of censorship on a number of occasions.

In fact, censorship is the first abuse of power that Beaumarchais criticises during Figaro's tirade against his bad luck at the theatre, in which he derisively compares censors to insects:

"Given over as they are to the mutual hatreds which spring from their ridiculous rivalries, all the various insects, flies, gnats, midges, critics, envious journalists, booksellers, publishers, the whole swarm of parasites attach themselves to the skin of the unfortunate man of letters and succeed in the end in sucking out of him what little bit of life and blood remain to him" (Act I, Scene II)

Beaumarchais also uses the character of Bartholo to criticise those who use the power they have

---

1. This quotation has been translated by BrightSummaries.com.

been granted in arbitrary, unfair and tyrannical ways:

> "YOUTHFUL: I ask you, Master, is it fair, is it right, is it just? [Sneezes.] BARTHOLO: Just? What has justice to do with miserable wretches like you? I'm your master, and what I say must be right." (Act II, Scene VII)

The main victim of Bartholo's tyranny is Rosine, who is locked up against her will and is almost forced to marry him, which is even against the law:

> "ROSINE: His wife! Me! Spend all my days with a jealous old man who can offer a young girl nothing but a life of horrible slavery!"(Act III, Scene XII)

Finally, Beaumarchais also uses the character of Bazile to criticise the corrupt and unscrupulous, who have no qualms about aiding the powerful to oppress whoever they wish:

> BAZILE: Calumny, Sir. You don't realize its effectiveness. I've seen the best of men pretty near overwhelmed by it. Believe me there's no spiteful stupidity, no horror, no absurd story that one can't get the idle-minded folk of a great

> city to swallow if one goes the right way about it." (Act II, Scene VIII)

By criticising the abuse of power in this way, Beaumarchais also extols the virtues of freedom of expression and the freedom to live and love without restraint. He is not seeking to challenge the established order, but rather to denounce the way the powerful misuse their power to the detriment of the weakest members of society. In *The Barber of Seville*, the characters who are the victims of misused power, namely Rosine and Figaro, are also the most cunning characters in the entire play, and display much more ingenuity and spirit than anyone else. This is Beaumarchais' way of declaring that gender and class cannot be used to judge someone's worth, nor can they be used to justify any abuse of power.

FURTHER REFLECTION

SOME QUESTIONS TO THINK ABOUT...

- Write a description of the character of Figaro. In what ways does he differ from the traditional archetype of a manservant?
- Which scenes in the play make it clear that Bazile is untrustworthy?
- Compare the ways that nobility (the Count) and the bourgeoisie (Don Bartholo) are portrayed in *The Barber of Seville*.
- Does *The Barber of Seville* adhere to the three unities of narrative and the rules of tone and decorum that govern classical drama?
- *The Barber of Seville* underwent multiple rewrites. Is this noticeable when reading the final version of the script? Explain your answer.
- Compare and contrast *The Barber of Seville* with *The School for Wives* by Molière, focusing on the structure and characters of each play.
- In his preface to the original French version of the play, Beaumarchais asserted that his

intention was to write a kind of "imbroglio", meaning a play with a complicated plot. In your opinion, is this an accurate description of *The Barber of Seville*?

- Georges Danton (French politician and revolutionary, 1759-1794) said in 1789 that "Figaro has killed the nobility". In your opinion, can Figaro be described as a revolutionary character? Justify your answer.
- In your opinion, does the play centre on practices which are respectful of human rights? Justify your answer.
- Compare and contrast *The Barber of Seville* with some modern comedies with similar themes. In what ways is this play distinctive or unique?

We want to hear from you!
Leave a comment on your online library
and share your favourite books on social media!

FURTHER READING

REFERENCE EDITION

- Beaumarchais, P.-A. (1964) *The Barber of Seville and The Marriage of Figaro*. Trans. Wood, J. London: Penguin.

REFERENCE STUDIES

- Beaumarchais, P.-A. (1959) *Le Barbier de Séville*. Paris: Larousse.

- Dauvin, S. (1981) *Le Barbier de Séville, Beaumarchais*. Paris: Hatier.

ADAPTATION

- *Il Barbiere di Siviglia*. (1816) [Opera]. Gioachino Rossini. Rome.

www.brightsummaries.com

Ebook EAN: 9782808010665

Paperback EAN: 9782808010689

Legal Deposit: D/2018/12603/271

This guide was written with the collaboration of Hélène Dupuis for the sections "A blend of tradition and innovation", "The art of comedy", "The play's title" and "Criticism of power and those who abuse it".

Cover: © Primento

Digital conception by Primento, the digital partner of publishers.